written by
Meeg Pincus

illustrated by
Alexander Vidal

COUGAR
CROSSING

How Hollywood's Celebrity Cougar Helped Build a Bridge for City Wildlife

Beach Lane Books • New York London Toronto Sydney New Delhi

P-22 is his name. (For real.)
P for puma. (Also called a mountain lion or cougar.)
22 for ID number. (More on that later.)

He paces. Muscles flex. Tail twitches. Famous letters loom above him in the night.

How did this mountain lion get *here*? To a park squeezed between three huge highways in America's second largest city?

How did he become P-22—the famous "Hollywood cougar"— and a hero for city wildlife?

Born in the Santa Monica Mountains, a national park area near the city of Los Angeles, P-22 faced his first big challenge at age two.

The time came for him to disperse—to leave home to find a territory of his own, claim it with claw swipes on the ground, and protect it to the death from cougar competitors.

But other males had already claimed every inch of these mountains. And the rumbling city bellowed below.

P-22 needed a way to get to more mountains with space to spare. But how?

The best bet: a bridge.

A big, wide *animal bridge*—a wildlife crossing—covered in trees and grass. This could connect the city's last natural spaces to more mountain ranges and open land up north.

But, sadly, no such wildlife crossing existed.

We tried for years to get a wildlife crossing constructed. But we didn't have the support we needed.

LA's puma population was on its own—and on the road to extinction!

So P-22 headed into the city.

Like a tourist, he strolled past Beverly Hills mansions
and Hollywood hot spots.

By some miracle, P-22 made it across two major freeways—
surviving *twenty lanes* of LA's legendary traffic.
He found himself in a green, hilly place with no other cougar scents around.
He couldn't go back. He couldn't go forward.

Swipe.

He claimed his spot there.

He stalked prey at night—
mostly deer, sometimes
a coyote or raccoon.

He hid from humans
and dozed during the day.

One night, P-22 caught scent of a human. He heard a
rustle in the brush and whipped his head around for
a look.

Too late. He felt a sharp pinprick in his haunch.

Sometimes P-22 scratched markings in
the dirt and planted his scent to attract a mate.

One day, after eating some small prey in the park,
P-22 started to feel sick.

His skin burned and itched.
His hair dropped off in clumps.
His eyes nearly swelled shut.
What was happening?

Feeling better many months later, P-22 wandered into
a neighborhood near the park.
     He discovered a cozy spot—calm and quiet, dark and dry—
and settled down for a snooze.

When he woke up: loud voices, bright lights . . .

After most of the harried humans finally headed home,
P-22 slinked back into the night.
He'd just lie low inside his park territory and try
to avoid any big challenges for a while.

Meanwhile, P-22 had become world famous!

Finally, more folks were caring about cougars and supporting the wildlife crossing!

However ... one spot inside the park enticed P-22
with its nightly sounds and scents.

Strange sounds and scrumptious scents of prey
he'd never heard or smelled before.

P-22 continued to avoid humans at all costs, as cougars do. Even on the day Griffith Park hosted flocks of his fans, he was probably sleeping on the other side of the park.

P-22 paces . . . perhaps more slowly
than he used to.

Late in his life span, he likely won't live long
enough to see the completed crossing.

But, thanks to him, it will be built to save
his cougar cousins and other wildlife.

Hollywood's celebrity cougar will forever be a
hero to city animals everywhere.
He spotlighted a message for us all:

Twenty Years of LA's Mountain Lions

P-22 in 2013.

2002: A team of National Park Service (NPS) scientists begins their Los Angeles area mountain lion study in Santa Monica Mountains National Recreation Area, which borders the city of LA and the Pacific Ocean. They start tagging pumas, the first one a dominant male: P-1.

2009: P-22 is born in the Santa Monica Mountains. His father is P-1.

2012: Wildlife biologist Miguel Ordeñana spots P-22 on Griffith Park remote cameras. His team calls the NPS team, whose field lead, cougar expert Jeff Sikich, finds and collars P-22.

2013: National Wildlife Federation's California regional executive director Beth Pratt launches the #SaveLACougars campaign to raise funds for a wildlife crossing in Liberty Canyon, over the 101 freeway—long considered by scientists as the best solution. *National Geographic* magazine runs Steve Winter's iconic photos of P-22, bringing global attention to his plight.

2014: P-22 becomes deathly ill with mange, after ingesting rat poison in his small prey. Jeff Sikich and the NPS team treat him and likely save his life.

2015: A worker discovers P-22 in the crawl space of a house next to Griffith Park, which becomes a big news story.

2016: P-22 kills as prey an elderly LA Zoo koala named Killarney (who liked to wander the ground at night). The zoo director supports P-22 and vows to better protect the zoo animals. The city of Los Angeles declares October 22 "P-22 Day," and the first annual P-22 Day festival is celebrated in Griffith Park. Researchers predict the area's cougars could become extinct within fifty years if nothing changes.

2018: Tagged pumas die from cars (P-23, likely P-49) and likely rodent poisoning (P-55). The NPS team finds two dens of cougar kittens—tagged P-66 to P-73—and a young male, tagged P-74. Wildfires tear through Southern California, threatening all the tagged cougars with nowhere to flee. P-22 and nine others survive, but young P-74 and another (P-64) die as a result of the fires. The California Department of Transportation moves forward into final design and engineering for the wildlife crossing at Liberty Canyon.

2019: More LA cougars are killed by cars (P-61), rodent poison (P-30 and P-47, likely P-53), and human hunting (P-38)—and more are tagged (P-75 to P-79). A law goes before California's legislature to ban certain rodent poisons deadly to wildlife predators.

2021–2024: The wildlife crossing at Liberty Canyon is projected to break ground in 2021 and be completed by 2024. It's slated to be the biggest animal bridge in the world!

More about Cougars and Crossings

Cougar Facts

- **Scientific name:** *Puma concolor*
- **Common names:** cougar, puma, mountain lion, panther, catamount (The most names of any animal in the world!)
- **Size:** 6 to 8 feet long and 70 to 160 pounds when full grown
- **Speed:** up to 50 mph
- **Jump length:** as long as 40 feet (That's a large school bus, front to back!)
- **Jump height:** up to 15 feet
- **Diet:** mostly deer (three to four a month) and occasionally smaller mammals such as raccoons and coyotes
- **Typical adult male cougar sole territory:** 150 square miles (P-22's home, Griffith Park, is only 9 square miles!)
- **Life span in the wild:** 8 to 12 years
- **Human sightings:** Rare. 90% of reported "mountain lion" sightings are actually bobcats!
- **Biggest risks to cougars:** habitat loss, cars, rodent poison (ingested by their smaller prey), and human hunters
- **Humans' risk from cougars:** extremely minimal (You're more likely to be struck by lightning than attacked by a cougar! They go out of their way to avoid humans.)

Wildlife Crossings, by the Numbers

LA's wildlife crossing will join thousands of bridges and tunnels built just for animals around the world. Wildlife crossings provide animals of all kinds safe access to food, shelter, and mates—and keep ecosystems intact (which benefits all of us!). These numbers tell you a bit more about why we need them:

Miles of public roads in the US: 4 million

US auto accidents involving large mammals each year: 1 to 2 million

People injured or killed in these accidents each year: 26,000

US wild animals (vertebrates) killed by cars each day: 1 million (including approximately 100 cougars each year in California)

Number of US states with wildlife crossings: 43 (and counting)

Number of continents with wildlife crossings: 6 (all except Antarctica)

Decade of first wildlife crossings constructed: 1950s (in France)

Number of animals using wildlife crossings daily across the globe: countless

Do Your Own Research

You can check the status of every tagged LA-area puma here: nps.gov/samo/learn/nature/pumapage.htm.

And check on LA's wildlife crossing here: www.savelacougars.org.

great horned owl

red-tailed hawk

acorn woodpecker

coyote

alligator lizard

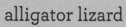

striped skunk

mountain lion

Wildlife of Southern California
Can you find them in this book?

Northern mockingbird

common poorwill

western grey squirrel

raccoon

canyon bat

mule deer

American black bear

California quail

desert cottontail

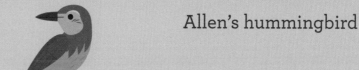

Allen's hummingbird

scrub jay

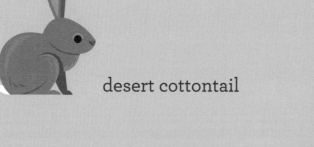

monarch butterfly

California ground squirrel

Author's Note

I love the idea of people building bridges and tunnels for animals. As I was researching to write a book about wildlife crossings around the world, I came across P-22. I couldn't believe how his predicament brought to life the struggles of so many urban and suburban animals and why we need wildlife crossings.

So, I dove into P-22's story, including interviewing amazing experts: the biologist who first tagged P-22 and leads the LA cougar study team (Jeff Sikich, National Park Service); the #SaveLACougars wildlife crossing campaign founder (Beth Pratt, National Wildlife Federation); and the biologist who first spotted P-22 and now supports the research and outreach efforts (Miguel Ordeñana, Natural History Museum of LA County [NHMLA]). I live a couple of hours down the coast from P-22, so I brought my family to visit Griffith Park and the P-22 exhibit at the NHMLA. This book grew to be about both P-22's journey and the need for wildlife crossings—and I hope it helps open hearts and eyes to the importance of protecting wild animals in our communities.

Selected Bibliography

Curwen, Thomas. "A Week in the Life of P-22, the Big Cat Who Shares Griffith Park with Millions of People." *Los Angeles Times*, February 8, 2017. http://www.latimes.com/projects/la-me-griffith-park-mountain-lion/ .

Hillard, Gloria. "LA Mountain Lion a Poster Cat for California's Rat Poison Problem." National Public Radio (NPR), June 21, 2014. https://www.npr.org/2014/06/21/323970068/la-mountain-lion-a-poster-cat-for-californias-rat-poison-problem.

Kaplan, Sarah. "L.A. Zoo to the Mountain Lion That Probably Ate Its Koala: No Hard Feelings." *Washington Post*, March 17, 2016. https://www.washingtonpost.com/news/morning-mix/wp/2016/03/17/l-a-zoo-to-the-mountain-lion-that-probably-ate-its-koala-no-hard-feelings/.

Ordeñana, Miguel. "An LA Story." *Earth Island Journal* (Summer 2016). http://www.earthisland.org/journal/index.php/eij/article/an_la_story/.

Pratt, Beth. "How a Lonely Cougar in Los Angeles Inspired the World." Lecture. TEDxYosemite video, 17:19, February 22, 2016. https://youtu.be/pMO8-f7onFY.

Pratt-Bergstrom, Beth. *When Mountain Lions Are Neighbors: People and Wildlife Working It Out in California*. Berkeley, CA: National Wildlife Federation and Heyday Press, 2016.

Solly, Meilan, "California Will Build the Largest Wildlife Crossing in the World." *Smithsonian Magazine*, August 21, 2019. https://www.smithsonianmag.com/smart-news/california-will-build-largest-wildlife-crossing-world-180972947/.

Vara, Kathy, and Asher Klein. "Mountain Lion P-22 'Left the Building' After Hours under House." NBC News, April 14, 2015. https://www.nbclosangeles.com/news/local/Mountain-Lion-Los-Feliz-Home-Crawl-Space-299608641.html.

For Amy McKenzie—LA lady, mama lion soul,
most amazing friend and auntie—always
—M. P.

For my nieces
—A. V.

BEACH LANE BOOKS • An imprint of Simon & Schuster Children's Publishing Division • 1230 Avenue of the Americas, New York, New York 10020 • Text copyright © 2021 by Meeg Pincus • Illustrations copyright © 2021 by Alexander Vidal • All rights reserved, including the right of reproduction in whole or in part in any form. • BEACH LANE BOOKS is a trademark of Simon & Schuster, Inc. • For information about special discounts for bulk purchases, please contact Simon & Schuster Special Sales at 1-866-506-1949 or business@simonandschuster.com. • The Simon & Schuster Speakers Bureau can bring authors to your live event. For more information or to book an event, contact the Simon & Schuster Speakers Bureau at 1-866-248-3049 or visit our website at www.simonspeakers.com. • Book design by Lauren Rille • The text for this book was set in Archer. • The illustrations for this book were rendered digitally. Manufactured in China • 1120 SCP • First Edition • 10 9 8 7 6 5 4 3 2 1 • CIP data for this book is available from the Library of Congress. • ISBN 978-1-5344-6185-7 • ISBN 978-1-5344-6186-4 (eBook)